J. RONALD TERWILLIGER
WORKFORCE HOUSING
MODELS OF
EXCELLENCE
AWARDS

"Those who serve their communities should be embraced by their communities . . . not shut out. I am making it my mission to engage the private sector to help solve this growing crisis."

J. Ronald Terwilliger, Chairman,
ULI Terwilliger Center for Workforce Housing

Urban Land Institute
1025 Thomas Jefferson Street, N.W., Suite 500 West
Washington, D.C. 20007-5201

ULI Catalog Number: B37
ISBN: 978-0-87420-141-3

Project Staff

Pamela H. Patenaude
Executive Director
ULI Terwilliger Center for Workforce Housing

Ashley Korb
Awards Project Coordinator
Manager
ULI Terwilliger Center for Workforce Housing

Richard M. Haughey
Publication Director
Senior Research Director
ULI Center for Balanced Development in the West

Patrick Pontius
Coauthor, Case Studies
Senior Research Associate
ULI Center for Balanced Development in the West

Theodore C. Thoerig
Coauthor, Case Studies
Senior Research Associate
Urban Land Institute

James A. Mulligan
Managing Editor/Manuscript Editor
Senior Editor
Urban Land Institute

Sharri Wolfgang
Designer
Auras Design

Betsy Van Buskirk
Creative Director
Urban Land Institute

Colleen DiPietro
Production Associate
Urban Land Institute

About the Urban Land Institute

The Urban Land Institute is a 501(c)(3) nonprofit research and education organization supported by its members. Founded in 1936, the Institute now has more than 38,000 members worldwide representing the entire spectrum of land use and real estate development disciplines, working in private enterprise and public service. As the preeminent, multidisciplinary real estate forum, ULI facilitates the open exchange of ideas, information, and experience among local, national, and international industry leaders and policy makers dedicated to creating better places.

The mission of the Urban Land Institute is to provide leadership in the responsible use of land and in creating and sustaining thriving communities worldwide. Members say ULI is a trusted idea place where leaders come to grow professionally and personally through sharing, mentoring, and problem solving. With pride, ULI members commit to the best in land use policy and practice.

About the ULI Terwilliger Center for Workforce Housing

The ULI Terwilliger Center for Workforce Housing was established by J. Ronald Terwilliger, chairman and CEO of Trammell Crow Residential, to expand housing opportunities for working families. The mission of the Center is to serve as a catalyst in increasing the availability of workforce housing in high-cost communities by harnessing the power of the private sector. The Center supports the development of mixed-income communities close to employment centers and transportation hubs. Through a multifaceted approach, the Center facilitates research, advocates for public policy change, publishes best practices, convenes housing experts, and works to eliminate regulatory barriers to the production of workforce housing.

The J. Ronald Terwilliger Models of Excellence Awards Program

ULI's J. Ronald Terwilliger Workforce Housing Models of Excellence Awards recognize and honor developers demonstrating leadership and creativity in providing expanded housing opportunities for America's working families. The awards celebrate exemplary developments that meet workforce housing needs in high-cost communities.

The awards jury, composed of the Terwilliger Center's National Advisory Board, evaluates developments based on the following criteria:

- **affordability**;
- **proximity to centers of employment and transportation hubs;**
- **quality of the design and site planning;**
- **involvement of public and private partnerships;**
- **use of regulatory reform to reduce costs;**
- **energy efficiency;**
- **sustainable green construction and land development;**
- **innovative building technologies and systems; and**
- **replicability of the development.**

Selection Process

- Applications are solicited via a call for entries distributed in March.
- Developers and/or other members of the development team submit completed applications to ULI's Terwilliger Center by a set deadline in June.
- A review panel composed of developers, ULI staff, and consultants convenes to evaluate the submissions and select applicants for site visits.
- Teams of two reviewers or jury members visit each selected site.
- When all site visits have been completed, the review panel reconvenes to select the final applicants to be submitted to the jury for final consideration.
- The jury convenes in October and chooses award winners and finalists.
- Award winners are announced at a ceremony at ULI's annual Fall Meeting.

Contents

JURY

2008

J. Ronald Terwilliger

TRAMMELL CROW RESIDENTIAL
Chairman of the Board

J. Ronald Terwilliger became chairman and chief executive officer of Trammell Crow Residential in 1986 and currently serves as chairman. Trammell Crow Residential is a national residential real estate company and is the largest developer of multifamily housing in the United States. Terwilliger is an honors graduate of the U.S. Naval Academy. After serving for five years in the Navy, he received his MBA degree with High Distinction from the Harvard Graduate School of Business and was elected a Baker Scholar.

Terwilliger currently chairs the board of Habitat for Humanity International and is a director of the Naval Academy Foundation. He is also a member of the executive committee for the Enterprise Community Partners board of trustees and chairman emeritus of the Wharton Real Estate Center of the University of Pennsylvania.

He is past chairman of the Urban Land Institute, where he served on the Governance Committee and remains a trustee, and is past chairman of the National Association of Homebuilders Multifamily Leadership Board.

In 2007, he made a $5 million gift to establish the ULI Terwilliger Center for Workforce Housing, and a $5 million gift to the Enterprise Foundation to create the Enterprise Terwilliger Fund for the development of affordable housing.

Terwilliger received the National Housing Conference 2009 Housing Person of the Year Award and was inducted into the National Association of Homebuilder's Hall of Fame in 2008 in recognition of his efforts to advance housing opportunities for all Americans.

He was honored by the U.S. Naval Academy with the 2009 Distinguished Graduate Award for his lifetime commitment to service, his personal character, and his contributions to the United States.

Robert C. Larson

LARSON REALTY GROUP
Chairman

Robert Larson is a principal and non-executive chairman of the Larson Realty Group. He is also a managing director and chairman of Lazard Frerès Real Estate Investors LLC, which provides global financial services, including banking, to corporations, partnerships, institutions, governments, and individuals.

Larson was a director of Intercontinental Hotels Group PLC, a global hospitality group based in London that operates more than 3,250 hotels in nearly 100 countries. He is also chairman of United Dominion Realty Trust Inc., one of the country's largest multifamily real estate companies, and a director of Brandywine Realty Trust, a real estate investment trust engaged in the development, ownership, and management of office and industrial properties in the Mid-Atlantic region. He also represents Lazard as a director of Atria Senior Living Group Inc., Destination Europe Ltd., Commonwealth Atlantic Properties Inc., and ARV Assisted Living Inc., and as a member of the Partnership Committee of DP Operating Partnership L.P.

A resident of Bloomfield Hills, Michigan, Larson's civic involvement includes serving as a director of the Greater Downtown Partnership Inc., the public/private organization established by former Mayor Dennis Archer to spearhead downtown revitalization and economic development in Detroit. He is also chairman emeritus of the advisory board of the Wharton Real Estate Center at the University of Pennsylvania, past chairman of the National Realty Committee, a Counselor of Real Estate (CRE), and a member of the Real Estate Roundtable.

Larson is chairman of the board of trustees of Cranbrook Educational Community, a trustee of Carleton College, a trustee of the Kresge Foundation, a trustee of the Detroit Medical Center, an honorary trustee and past chairman of the National Urban League, a trustee of Children's Hospital of Michigan, a governor of Cranbrook Academy of Art, and a director of Spoleto Festival USA.

Bart Harvey

ENTERPRISE
Former Chairman and CEO

Bart Harvey took over leadership of Enterprise Community Partners in 1993 from cofounder James W. Rouse after close to ten years of working with him to further the organization's mission. During Harvey's 13-year tenure as chairman and CEO, Enterprise grew into a leading provider of development capital and expertise to create decent, affordable homes and to rebuild communities. Enterprise has raised and invested $7 billion in equity, grants, and loans and is currently investing in communities at a rate of $1 billion per year, providing more than 215,000 affordable homes to low-income families and individuals.

Rouse and Harvey are credited with working with Congress to help create the Low-Income Housing Tax Credit, which provides the financing for the vast majority of affordable rental homes in this country. In 2004, Enterprise created the $555 million Green Communities initiative, which is responsible for the construction of more than 8,500 affordable, environmentally sustainable homes.

Before joining Rouse at Enterprise in 1984, Harvey was managing director of corporate finance for investment bank Dean Witter Reynolds. He also served with Rouse on the National Housing Task Force and was appointed to the Mitchell-Danforth Task Force on the Low-Income Housing Tax Credit. In 2002, he was appointed by Congress to the Millennial Housing Commission and has served on a number of boards, including for the Federal Home Loan Bank of Atlanta. Harvey's civic involvement includes serving on the boards of Keswick Multi-Care Center Foundation, the Baltimore Educational Trust, Bright Horizons Family Solutions, Center Stage, Shepherd's Clinic, and the Harvard Alumni Association. He testifies often before Congress on a number of community development–related issues and has been published in numerous journals and periodicals. He holds bachelor's and master's degrees from Harvard University.

Bruce Katz

THE BROOKINGS INSTITUTION
Vice President/Founding Director of the
Brookings Metropolitan Policy Program

Bruce Katz regularly advises national, state, regional, and municipal leaders on policy reforms that advance the competitiveness of metropolitan areas. He focuses particularly on reforms that promote the revitalization of central cities and older suburbs and enhance the ability of these places to attract, retain, and expand the middle class. The Brookings Metropolitan Policy Program, of which Katz is the founding director, seeks to redefine the challenges facing cities and metropolitan areas by publishing cutting-edge research on major demographic, market, development, and governance trends. In 2006, he received the Heinz Award in Public Policy for his contributions to urban and metropolitan America.

Katz is a frequent writer and commentator on urban and metropolitan issues. He is the editor or coeditor of several books on transportation, demographics, and regionalism, including *Taking the High Road* (Brookings Press, 2005), *Redefining Urban and Suburban America* (Brookings Press, 2003), and *Reflections on Regionalism* (Brookings Press, 2000). His op-eds and articles have appeared in a wide range of major national and regional newspapers, including *Atlantic Monthly*, *Washington Post*, *Los Angeles Times*, *Christian Science Monitor*, *Boston Globe*, *BusinessWeek*, *Philadelphia Inquirer*, and *Baltimore Sun*. Katz frequently appears on TV and radio, including National Public Radio's *Morning Edition*, PBS's *NewsHour*, and CNN.

He is also a visiting professor of social policy at the London School of Economics. Before joining Brookings, Katz was chief of staff to Henry G. Cisneros, former secretary of Housing and Urban Development. He also was staff director of the Senate Subcommittee on Housing and Urban Affairs. Katz is a graduate of Brown University and Yale Law School.

Jack Kemp

KEMP PARTNERS
Founder and Chairman

Jack Kemp is founder and chairman of Kemp Partners, a strategic consulting firm that seeks to provide clients with strategic counsel, relationship development, and marketing advice, helping them accomplish business and policy objectives. He is cochair of the Lincoln Bicentennial Cabinet, a group formed by the Abraham Lincoln Bicentennial Commission to support its public/private efforts.

Kemp was cochair of the Council on Foreign Relations' Russia Task Force and codirector of Empower America. He served on House Speaker Dennis Hastert's Saving America's Cities Working Group, and helped form a nonpartisan, nonprofit think tank, the Foundation for the Defense of Democracies. He also writes a weekly nationally syndicated column for the Copley News Service.

Kemp received the Republican Party's nomination for vice president in 1996 and was chairman of the National Commission on Economic Growth and Tax Reform. He served four years as secretary of Housing and Urban Development (HUD) in the George H.W. Bush Administration and was the author of the Enterprise Zones legislation to encourage entrepreneurship and job creation in urban America.

Before his appointment as HUD secretary, Kemp represented the Buffalo area and western New York for 18 years in the U.S. House of Representatives. He served for seven years in the Republican leadership as chairman of the House Republican Conference. Before his election to Congress, Kemp played 13 years as a professional football quarterback; he was captain of the San Diego Chargers and the Buffalo Bills.

Kemp has been a director of Oracle since 1995 and a key strategic adviser to many corporations. He is on the board of Hawk Corp. and Six Flags and is an advisory board member of Toyota's Diversity initiative, Thayer Capital in Washington, and Thomas Weisel Partners, a merchant banking firm in San Francisco.

Rick Lazio

JP MORGAN ASSET MANAGEMENT
Managing Director

Rick Lazio, who has been with JP Morgan since 2004, currently serves as managing director of the Global Real Estate and Infrastructure Team, where he focuses on client development and marketing to investors, strengthening relationships with governmental and other public officials, and advising clients and the firm on public policy issues. Previously, Lazio was executive vice president of global government affairs and public policy at JPMorgan Chase and a member of the executive committee. Before joining the firm, Lazio for three years was president and chief executive officer of the Financial Services Forum, an economic policy organization composed of CEOs of 20 of the largest financial institutions doing business in the United States.

Lazio was elected to the U.S. Congress in 1992 and represented New York's 2nd District for four terms. He became deputy majority whip in 1995 and was later assistant majority leader. He served on both the House Commerce and Banking committees during the drafting and passage of the Gramm-Leach-Bliley Financial Services Modernization Act of 1999 and was chair of the Banking Committee's Subcommittee on Housing. In 1984, he became an assistant district attorney in Suffolk County, New York, serving for five years before being elected to the Suffolk County Legislature. He also was chairman of the Audit Committee of TB Woods Corporation, as well as chair of the Polaroid Company Governance Committee.

He is on the boards of the World Rehabilitation Fund, Audubon New York, Enterprise Community Partners, the Ad Council, Committee for Economic Development, and International Conservation Caucus Foundation. Lazio holds a bachelor's degree from Vassar College and a law degree from American University, and has received two honorary doctorates.

Nicolas P. Retsinas

HARVARD UNIVERSITY'S
JOINT CENTER FOR HOUSING STUDIES
Director

Nicolas Retsinas is director of Harvard University's Joint Center for Housing Studies, a collaborative venture of the Graduate School of Design and the Harvard Kennedy School. The center conducts research to examine and address the most critical housing and community development issues in America. Retsinas is a lecturer in housing studies at the Graduate School of Design and the Harvard Kennedy School, and a lecturer in real estate at the Harvard Business School.

Before his appointment, Retsinas was assistant secretary for housing/federal housing commissioner at the U.S. Department of Housing and Urban Development and was director of the Office of Thrift Supervision. He also was on the board of the Federal Deposit Insurance Corporation, the Federal Housing Finance Board, and the Neighborhood Reinvestment Corporation. Retsinas was executive director of the Rhode Island Housing and Mortgage Finance Corporation from 1987 to 1993 and is on the board of trustees of the National Housing Endowment and Enterprise Community Partners. He is on the board of directors of ShoreBank, Community Development Trust Inc., and the Center for Responsible Lending. He is the immediate past chair of the board of directors of Habitat for Humanity International.

Retsinas is coauthor of *Our Communities, Our Homes: Pathways to Housing and Homeownership in America's Cities and States* (2007).

Retsinas is a fellow at the National Academy for Public Administration and the Urban Land Institute. Retsinas was named one of the most influential people in real estate by the National Association of Realtors, *Builder* magazine, and *Multi-Housing News*. He holds a master's degree in city planning from Harvard University and a bachelor's degree in economics from New York University.

National Advisory Board

Project Site Reviewers

PHYLLIS ALZAMORA
Executive Director
ULI Orange County

RAYMOND CHRISTMAN
Chairman
Peachtree Corridor Partnership

ELIZABETH DAVISON
Consultant
Washington, D.C.

JEFFREY DUFRESNE
Executive Director
ULI Atlanta

DAVID ENGEL
Consultant
Washington, D.C.

TAYLOR GRANT
President
California Real Estate Receiverships

RICHARD M. HAUGHEY
Senior Research Director
Urban Land Institute

SHALLEY JONES HORN
Director
Office of Community and Economic
Development, Miami Dade County

ASHLEY KORB
Manager
ULI Terwilliger Center for Workforce Housing

DANIEL McGRAIN
Principal
McGrain Realty Advisors

JOHN McKINNERNEY
Partner
Simmons, Vedder & Company

PAMELA H. PATENAUDE
Executive Director
ULI Terwilliger Center for Workforce Housing

J. MICHAEL PITCHFORD
President and CEO
Community Preservation and Development
Corporation

THEODORE C. THOERIG
Senior Research Associate
Urban Land Institute

KATE WHITE
Executive Director
ULI San Francisco

WINNERS

THE 2008 J. RONALD TERWILLIGER WORKFORCE HOUSING MODELS OF EXCELLENCE AWARDS

2008

CITYVIEW • JOHN LAING HOMES

BOULEVARD IN ANAHEIM

ANAHEIM, CALIFORNIA

DEVELOPERS

CityView,
Los Angeles, California

John Laing Homes,
Irvine, California

**HOUSING
INFORMATION**

36 For-Sale Townhomes

20 For-Sale Single-
Family Detached Homes

AFFORDABILITY

28 Townhouses
(80–120% of AMI)

8 Townhouses
(Below 60% of AMI)

20 Single-Family
Detached Homes
(Market Rate)

Located in downtown Anaheim, California, a community with a large housing affordability gap, the Boulevard in Anaheim consists of 36 attached townhouses—all of which are income restricted—and 20 market-rate single-family homes. The development of the residential community benefited from a strong public/private partnership between the developers—John Laing Homes and CityView—and the Anaheim Redevelopment Agency, and also from a number of policy tools designed to facilitate the production of workforce housing. At the corner of two major downtown streets, the infill redevelopment plays a visible role in the city's efforts to change the industrial and automotive character of the area adjoining downtown and to fulfill its greater goal of encouraging creation of walkable, affordable, and sustainable communities throughout Anaheim.

"Creating a model that works for for-profit homebuilders is the key to bringing about large-scale production of workforce housing and solving our workforce housing problem. The Boulevard in Anaheim represents such a model, which could be replicated in communities across the country." Rick Lazio

Community Information

Anaheim, California, is home to an estimated 346,832 people, making it the tenth-most-populous city in California and the second-largest municipality in Orange County. It is part of the southern California megalopolis—a vast, 10,000-square-mile area encompassing Los Angeles and San Diego with a population that is approaching 20 million.

Anaheim's largest industry is tourism, with the Disneyland Resort, the Anaheim Convention Center (the largest on the West Coast), Angel Stadium of Anaheim, and dozens of hotels, all located within the city limits. The city's three largest employers—the Walt Disney Company, Orange County, and the University of California at Irvine—draw a labor pool composed largely of service industry workers, teachers, and municipal employees.

Workforce Housing Problem

Even with recent housing price declines, California has a shortage of housing affordable to most working families. According to the California Association of Realtors First Time Buyer Affordability Index, 64 percent of households in Orange County cannot afford an entry-level home in the county. In Anaheim, the workforce housing deficit is severe: the city's median home price of $588,500 is more than ten times greater than its median household income of $52,087 for a family of four. With incomes and housing prices separated by a large gap, homeownership is beyond the means of many residents. Local workers, many of whom work in the dominant tourism industry, are forced to endure long commutes to afford suitable housing, a problem the city has mobilized to resolve.

Community Response

The city of Anaheim views its affordability gap as an important issue that threatens its local economy by making the city less competitive with markets that have more available afford-able housing. Because city leaders realize there is no single solution to the problem, they employ a variety of tools, often in concert, to encourage development of workforce housing, including brownfield cleanup, redevelopment overlay zones, land writedowns, second mortgages, and homeownership education programs for potential homeowners. The city saw the large tracts of brownfield industrial land located adjacent to downtown as a prime redevelopment opportunity and a chance to leverage affordable and workforce housing in a pedestrian-oriented community that would be within walking distance of the amenities of downtown Anaheim. Through creation of a redevelopment overlay zone, the city created incentives for redevelopment, including environ-mental remediation and land writedowns. The Boulevard in Anaheim is one community within the redevelopment area, which along with other projects in the district is spurring an economic renais-sance in the area, creating value for the new homeowners.

Project Specifics and Affordability

Completed in July 2005, the Boulevard in Anaheim comprises 36 attached townhouses reserved as workforce and affordable housing and 20 market-rate single-family homes. Of the 36 reserved units, 28 were reserved for households with incomes from 80 to 120 percent of the area median income (AMI) and eight were reserved for low-income households with incomes below 60 percent of the AMI. The 5.5-acre community is located on a former truck transfer facility downtown in the

The city's three largest employers—the Walt Disney Company, Orange County, and the University of California at Irvine— draw a labor pool composed largely of service industry workers, teachers, and municipal employees.

Anaheim Colony Historic District. The infill project is adjacent to an existing single-family neighborhood and is bounded on the north by an existing rail line that runs down the middle of Santa Ana Street and on the east by Anaheim Boulevard, a major corridor to downtown Anaheim. With its proximity to major employment centers, including City Hall, Disneyland, and the Anaheim Convention Center, and varied transportation options—bus service, major freeways, and Metrolink—the Boulevard in Anaheim fulfills the city's mission of creating pedestrian-friendly, affordable residential communities.

The workforce units at the Boulevard in Anaheim were priced at $305,000 to $341,000, and more than 3,000 families applied for the opportunity to purchase a townhouse. To qualify for the workforce housing units, households must earn 80 to 120 percent of the AMI—$67,280 to $100,920, based on the AMI of $84,100. The market-rate residences were designed to sell for less than the median home price in Anaheim. While the pro forma estimated that single-family homes would sell in the low $500,000s, they ultimately sold for over $600,000, signaling market acceptance of the project and improving the overall financial performance of the development. With the enormous pent-up demand for workforce and affordable for-sale housing in Orange County, all the workforce townhouses were sold before completion. The market-rate single-family residences benefited from a red-hot housing market in southern California and sold out quickly.

Land and Site Acquisition

The Boulevard in Anaheim was the result of an extensive public/private partnership—from site acquisition through homebuyer financing—between the developers and the Anaheim Redevelopment Agency. The project site was owned by the city. Capitalizing on the opportunity to create the first new residential community in this area since the 1940s, the city offered to assist in the environmental cleanup and land acquisition of the site in exchange for the development of workforce units.

Encouraged by a land writedown by the city, the developers acquired the site for $3.6 million in July 2003. It was known that the site was contaminated by diesel particulates from its earlier use as a truck transfer facility and would require extensive remediation before construction could begin. The environmental cleanup was accomplished through the joint efforts of the Anaheim Redevelopment Agency and the development team, and was supported by the U.S. Environmental Protection Agency (EPA). The project was also the first in Orange County to use the Polanco Redevelopment Act, legislation enacted to help limit the uncertainty of liability often associated with environmental remediation. Because the site was publicly owned, it qualified under the legislation for immunity protection and the issuance of indemnities to the builder.

Planning Entitlements and Development

To encourage redevelopment of the site, the city created an overlay zone to spur the private sector to create a walkable, affordable community. In exchange for municipal assistance with environmental remediation, off-site improvements, and land acquisition, the city established a prerequisite that workforce housing be incorporated in any future development. The indirect supply-side subsidies provided by the Anaheim Redevelopment Agency afforded the developers the financial flexibility to pursue the project.

More than ten community meetings were held to ensure that the project successfully blended into the neighborhood fabric. While the site was bound by Santa Ana and Anaheim streets,

It was known that the site was contaminated by diesel particulates from its earlier use as a truck transfer facility and would require extensive remediation before construction could begin.

with commercial uses across the street, it abutted a residential neighborhood designated as the Anaheim Colony Historic District. The community meetings focused on making sure the new single-family homes were successfully integrated with the community, including using a variety of architectural styles reflected in the existing community. The city also committed to a number of improvements in the immediate area, among them the upgrade of Anaheim Boulevard.

Financing

John Laing Homes, a developer with decades of homebuilding experience in the region, teamed with CityView, which has extensive experience in financing workforce housing in traditionally underserved markets. CityView partners with production builders, which allows for large- and small-scale production of mixed-income communities providing housing for families with a wide range of incomes. With the right location and product, the market-rate housing can be constructed for a price that qualifies it as workforce housing.

The ability to combine market-rate units with workforce townhouses—in effect cross-subsidizing the project and the writedown of land costs—made the project financially feasible for the developers. The anticipated sale price of the market-rate residences provided financial flexibility, allowing development of over 65 percent of the project as workforce housing. While the timing helped the project achieve financial success—the single-family homes were brought to market during the peak of the housing boom—the phased construction was also beneficial, according to the developer.

Second mortgages were offered by the city through its second mortgage assistance program (SMAP). The city provided $75,000 mortgages with 3 percent interest for the low-income buyers and $50,000 mortgages with a 5 percent interest rate for the moderate-income buyers. The second mortgages usually removed the private mortgage insurance requirements of the primary loan.

Design, Construction, and Sustainability

As one of the state's older cities, Anaheim has a downtown that boasts a more traditional urban form than its southern California counterparts. The infill project is located in the Anaheim Colony Historic District, the boundaries of which delineate the original town founded in 1857. Within the historic district, more than 1,100 contributing structures represent a variety of architectural styles such as Victorian, mission revival, and Arts and Crafts.

Anaheim's Second Mortgage Assistance Program

In 1988, the Anaheim city council passed a resolution approving the Second Mortgage Assistance Program (SMAP), and to date, the program has provided over 400 second mortgage loans to working families. The program is funded by a 20 percent set-aside in conjunction with the designated redevelopment areas. In California, cities can designate blighted areas and can set aside 20 percent of the tax increment gain from those areas each year for housing.

The program functions in a way similar to other "soft second" loans: qualifying buyers obtain a public loan from the city to apply to their downpayment; the loan amount is treated as equity and gets repaid from the proceeds of any future sale. Homeownership options are opened to individuals who otherwise would not qualify for traditional lending. SMAP recipients can apply their funds to almost any property in the city and enjoy full property appreciation. However, in some cases—specifically when the housing affordability was a direct result of city investment—the city will mandate an equity split in any price appreciation upon resale. While a homeowner can choose to make payments on the second mortgage during the life of the loan, no repayment is required until property resale.

To qualify for an SMAP loan, applicants must be legal U.S. residents, complete a U.S. Department of Housing and Urban Development–certified homebuyer education course, and meet certain income requirements. Currently, there is a long waiting list for SMAP loans and priority goes to residents displaced by city redevelopment projects, followed by those who reside or work in Anaheim. In addition to the 20 percent set-aside, loan repayments are returned to the program, making it essentially a revolving loan fund.

The site design of the Boulevard in Anaheim reflects new urbanist principles: minimal setbacks, front porches and stoops, and rear-loading garages with access from an alleyway. The project has ample sidewalks lined with large trees—some of which were retained during construction—and extensive landscaping. The attractive design and thoughtful layout of the project allows it to avoid any stigma sometimes associated with affordable housing. The community has the appearance of a full market-rate community.

One of the design team's foremost challenges was to ensure that the building design was compatible with the character of the historic district, especially the single-family homes adjacent to the site. Input from the many community meetings led to architectural changes to the single-family homes and visual separation from the townhouses through additional landscaping.

The residential units at the Boulevard in Anaheim are spacious by California standards; the workforce units—which range from 1,370 to 1,870 square feet—are much larger than those found in comparable projects. All residences feature Energy Star appliances and low-flow plumbing fixtures. While the project planning preceded the mainstream emergence of the U.S. Green Building

Council's Leadership in Energy and Environmental Design (LEED) certification process, the residential community exceeds California's Title 24 energy efficiency standards.

Management and Affordability Controls

When owners of income-restricted units sell, they have two choices: to sell at the new affordable price as calculated by the city, based on Housing and Community Development formulas, or to sell at the prevailing market rate. If they sell at the affordable price, the second mortgage and interest are due upon sale. The loan is also assumable by the new buyer, and the unit remains an income-restricted affordable unit. If they sell at the prevailing market rate, the second mortgage and interest are due upon sale, and any equity after repayment must be split evenly with the city. While this means the unit is lost as an income-restricted affordable unit, the city does receive 50 percent of the appreciation, which is directed back into the production or preservation of affordable housing in the city. Priority for sale of the workforce units was given to Anaheim residents and city employees; as a result, the majority of homeowners are residents who previously rented elsewhere in Anaheim.

Anaheim also requires that all SMAP buyers at the Boulevard in Anaheim attend a two-day homeownership workshop and obtain only 30-year, fixed-rate mortgages. Despite mounting foreclosures in the region due to the deteriorating housing situation, SMAP buyers citywide have experienced low default rates—a fact Anaheim attributes to its required homebuyer education.

Replication

The use of indirect supply-side subsidies—assistance with cleanup costs, land writedowns, and redevelopment overlay districts—is a replicable model for public agencies to ensure the inclusion of workforce housing in traditional development. Many cities with brownfield industrial land could create opportunities for new workforce housing in their communities through these techniques. In turn, the Boulevard in Anaheim provides an example of how a developer can use market-rate development to cross-subsidize workforce housing, creating an attractive, profitable product without the use of traditional direct public subsidies. And last, a demand-side second mortgage assistance program provides an effective tool to help working families bridge the downpayment gap that often keeps them from owning a home.

LEGACY AT LINCOLN PARK

ROCKVILLE, MARYLAND

DEVELOPERS

Urban Atlantic,
Bethesda, Maryland

Rockville Housing
Enterprises,
Rockville, Maryland

**HOUSING
INFORMATION**

53 For-Sale Townhouses

AFFORDABILITY

22 Townhouses
(80–120% of AMI)

10 Townhouses
(60–80% of AMI)

8 Townhouses
(Below 60%)

13 Townhouses
(Market Rate)

Legacy at Lincoln Park was completed on the site of a former public housing project in May 2008. Rockville Housing Enterprises and lead developer Urban Atlantic Development Inc. partnered to redevelop the site using a better housing model. For-sale housing was developed for households with a wide range of incomes. The community includes 53 townhouses, 40 of which are income-restricted.

Community Information

Located in Montgomery County, Maryland, several miles outside Washington, D.C., Rockville is an edge city with a dense, transit-oriented town center. Once an agricultural village, Rockville now is a first-tier suburb of Washington and has stations for both the Washington Metropolitan Area Transit Authority (Metro) rail system and Maryland Area Regional Commuter (MARC) trains, offering easy access to employment centers in Montgomery County and the District of Columbia. Almost 60,000 people reside within Rockville's 13.4 square miles; Montgomery County as a whole has more than 930,000 residents. With a small historic district, an excellent school system, and a pedestrian town center, Rockville affords a high quality of life.

Workforce Housing Problem

Given Rockville's status as a desirable close-in suburb, market demand for housing far outpaces supply. The median price is $540,000 for an existing single-family home in the county, and over $1 million for a new single-family home. While the American Community Survey reports that the county has a median income topping $87,000, homeownership is out of reach for many of its working families. Many of Rockville's teachers, nurses, police officers, and other vital municipal workers must commute from outside the county to find housing they can afford.

Community Response

Lincoln Terrace was an obsolete, 65-unit public housing complex in Lincoln Park, a historic working-class African American neighborhood about five blocks from downtown. Only 50 of its units were occupied, and many residents hoped to find other housing due to the poor condition of the facilities. Recognizing the need to redevelop the blighted site and create a new type of development that would provide housing for people with a mix of incomes, local neighborhood activists approached Rockville Housing Enterprises (RHE), the Rockville housing and redevelopment agency, to issue a request for proposals (RFP) for the demolition and redevelopment of Lincoln Terrace. The RFP included requirements to accommodate low-income residents. In a competitive process, the city of Rockville and RHE selected Urban Atlantic as the lead developer because of its willingness to develop mixed-income homeownership, which was the strong preference of the surrounding community.

Project Specifics and Affordability

Urban Atlantic in August 2003 acquired the development rights to Lincoln Terrace from RHE and the U.S. Department of Housing and Urban Development (HUD), and began work on demolition and redevelopment. Completed in May 2008, Legacy at Lincoln Park consists of 60 units and a public park. It contains 53 three-bedroom, three-bath townhouses, and seven four-bedroom, three-bath single-family detached homes. All units are fee-simple for sale. Of the 53 townhouses, eight are designated for low-income residents earning less than 60 percent of AMI, ten are for low- and moderate-income residents earning 60 to 80 percent of AMI, 22 are workforce units for those earning 80 to 120 percent of AMI, and 13 are market-rate units targeted at buyers earning more than 100 percent of AMI. All seven single-family detached homes are market rate.

The city of Rockville administers a moderately priced dwelling unit (MPDU) program (see page 26), which is similar to the well-known MPDU program of Montgomery County. The city program issues a certificate of eligibility to households with qualifying incomes; the certificate, good for one year, can be used to purchase an MPDU residence or to rent an affordable MPDU apartment. The city recognizes certificates from the county in its program and maintains a waiting list.

Through the rezoning process, MPDU requirements stipulated that Urban Atlantic set aside 12 percent of the units at prices affordable to families earning less than 60 percent of AMI. These units are required to maintain affordability levels for 30 years. The eight MPDU low-income units are priced at $200,000 to $225,000. The ten low- and moderate-income units have first mortgages of $250,000 for those households between 60 and 80 percent of AMI, and $340,000 for workforce housing for households in the 80 to 120 percent of AMI bracket. All the townhouses provide identical space and amenities, with the exception of the city-regulated MPDUs, which are priced at the same value as the market-rate townhouses. Affordability is bridged through second mortgages that are due on sale or refinance. The market-rate townhouses are priced at $438,000 and the market-rate single-family detached homes at $599,000.

While the American Community Survey reports that the county has a median income topping $87,000, homeownership is out of reach for many of its working families.

Land and Site Acquisition

The former Lincoln Terrace, the site of Legacy at Lincoln Park, was owned by RHE and restricted for development by HUD covenants. The Lincoln Park area of east Rockville has a long and rich history dating from 1891 as a center of Rockville's African American community. However, the Lincoln Terrace public housing complex had become a blight on its surrounding historic neighborhood. In order to preserve the heritage of the neighborhood and create an economically integrated community, RHE and the community supported redevelopment of the site as a mixed-income neighborhood consistent with the larger Lincoln Park neighborhood conservation plan.

Planning Entitlements and Development

RHE selected Urban Atlantic as a development partner. Together they developed a comprehensive program for relocation, job training, homeownership and credit counseling, financing, design, and creation of income tiers for the site. Urban Atlantic developed a program for using market-rate sales to subsidize low-income homeownership, while the workforce housing was developed to break even. The broad income tiers were made possible through the use of new and existing affordable housing tools, including the MPDU program, Section 8 housing vouchers, second mortgages, and below-market-rate financing from the Maryland Community Development Administration. The zoning process required the project meet only the 12 percent MPDU standard, but the program proposed and implemented by Urban Atlantic and RHE went well beyond that minimum by providing a higher number and wider variety of low- and moderate-income and workforce housing. After extensive demolition and site remediation, Urban Atlantic built new gas, water, and sewer lines to the site, as well as an oversize stormwater management facility that benefited the city by helping mitigate downstream flooding. The city assisted the development by accepting a transfer of the park land, the stormwater management facility, and other common areas and accepting permanent responsibility for their maintenance and operation.

Financing

Legacy at Lincoln Park's financial feasibility was achieved through the creative use of the land as collateral for the predevelopment and construction loans. RHE used the market value of the land to demonstrate equity and collateral to the lender, subordinating its interest to the predevelopment and construction loans. In this way, no additional private equity was required for the deal. The lenders had the right to call the land at a market value of about $5 million, while its value for mixed-income housing was substantially lower. The RHE land value was obtained through a cash purchase price upon sale of each unit, participation in the development fees, and acquisition of second mortgages for the difference between the serviceable first debt and the market value. These must-pay second mortgages are accrued and deferred mortgages and are due upon sale or refinance.

The Lincoln Park area of east Rockville has a long and rich history dating from 1891 as a center of Rockville's African American community. However, the Lincoln Terrace complex had become a blight.

Montgomery County's Moderately Priced Dwelling Unit Ordinance

One of the first and most successful inclusionary zoning programs in the country, Montgomery County's moderately priced dwelling unit (MPDU) program requires most new development to include an affordable component. The program has led to a dispersal of housing units throughout the county and provided low- to moderate-income families access to high-quality communities and services. The MPDU program's mandatory inclusionary zoning requires developers to reserve up to 15 percent of all newly constructed units for affordable housing. Montgomery County imposes strict income limits to accommodate first-time renters and buyers earning $16,000 to $49,000 for a family of four. Buyers and renters of MPDUs must undergo a background check and an education course. The MPDU units include a ten-year price restriction on for-sale homes and a 20-year restriction on rental units. Sales within the price restriction period adhere to MPDU pricing; sales after the ten-year period result in a profit split between the owner and the county. The county adjusts annually the price restriction guidelines to accommodate changes in inflation, cost of living, and construction costs.

The Montgomery County Council unanimously approved the MPDU legislation in 1973 in response to mounting resident concern regarding rising home prices. While aimed at mitigating affordability issues, it has never been a social welfare program. The target recipients of MPDUs are moderate-income professionals such as police officers, teachers, and municipal employees who otherwise could not afford to live in the communities in which they work. The county's Department of Housing and Community Affairs administers the program. It requires that any developments composed of more than 35 units located in areas zoned for lots covering a half acre or less must set aside 15 percent of built units for the MPDU program. The units must be mixed in with and indistinguishable on the exterior

from market-rate units. In general, MPDU status is tied to an individual unit and cannot be floated between units within a development. Of the for-sale MPDU units, 40 percent must be made available as rental units to the Housing Opportunities Commission (HOC), which administers the county's public housing subsidy programs. Developers participating in the MPDU program may receive a 20 percent density bonus. These bonuses are subject to approval by the Planning Board and are occasionally denied because of height restrictions or environmental or neighborhood concerns.

To date, more than 11,500 dwelling units have been produced under the program. While the MPDU program has enjoyed tremendous success, it faces a longevity challenge in that the units' affordability expires. If new development does not occur, and, hence, new MPDUs are not provided, Montgomery County will lose its ability to provide affordable housing for its workforce. As the county approaches buildout, it will rely more on denser multifamily infill development and preservation of existing units to address its affordability problems.

Design, Planning, and Sustainability

Given the heritage of Lincoln Park and the neighborhood's proximity to Rockville's dynamic mixed-use town center, the community wanted the redevelopment of Lincoln Terrace to revitalize the area. RHE, Urban Atlantic, and the Lincoln Park Civic Association solicited community involvement and feedback in the planning process. The resulting high level of community participation contributed to the specified mixed-income housing program and complementary architectural design that blends the project seamlessly into the neighborhood. Legacy's 60 units match the traditional height, scale, and style of the neighborhood. Further, the market-rate units in Legacy are indistinguishable from the income-restricted units.

In addition to achieving architectural compatibility, Legacy also increased the amount of green space in the neighborhood and alleviated flood problems. Urban Atlantic worked closely with the Rockville Recreation and Parks Forestry Division to map out all mature trees, resulting in a site plan focused on preserving trees, open space, and natural drainage paths. Rather than place the community at the center of the site, Urban Atlantic clustered the homes along a spine road. This design minimizes the amount of nonporous paved surfaces and maintains the site's natural grading. Urban Atlantic also planted trees and created a large, nearly one-acre park, as well as a stormwater management pond. The development team created this public, natural space by clustering the homes in an appropriate manner. The clustering of the homes, use of three-story heights and tuck-under parking, and a reduction in density—from 65 to 60 units—help the new homes blend with the surrounding community. The developers also improved the energy efficiency of the units, providing Energy Star appliances and low-flow water fixtures in each unit. Legacy also won a sustainability award from the Maryland National Capital Building Industry Association and the Maryland Department of Natural Resources.

The high level of community participation contributed to the mixed-income housing program and complementary architectural design that blends the project seamlessly into the neighborhood.

"What appealed to me about the Legacy at Lincoln Park community was that it was able to accomplish many of the goals of HOPE VI without the use of HOPE VI funds. The use of the land as collateral and subordinating it for the predevelopment and construction loans was creative and key to the success of this impressive project." Jack Kemp

Management and Affordability Controls

The MPDU townhouses have a 30-year holding guarantee. Rockville also contributed to the long-term affordability of the community by assuming responsibility for maintenance of the stormwater facility and the community park, thereby reducing homeowners association operating expenses and liability.

Replication

Displaced residents of the community were given comprehensive relocation assistance; job, credit, and homeownership counseling; and housing choice vouchers to assist with rental or homeownership throughout the city and county. Of the 50 families at Lincoln Terrace, 15 requested relocation and were successfully moved to other public housing in east Rockville, and 35 received vouchers and found new residences in the city. From a project perspective, Legacy offers a replicable example of redeveloping any publicly owned parcel of land. If developers partner with public agencies willing to employ innovative techniques—such as Rockville's land equity deal—then cities and developers can contribute to a better built environment.

THE COMMUNITY BUILDERS

MORGAN WOODS

EDGARTOWN, MASSACHUSETTS

DEVELOPER

The Community
Builders,
Boston, Massachusetts

**HOUSING
INFORMATION**

60 Rental Apartments

AFFORDABILITY

24 Apartments
(60–140% AMI)

30 Apartments
(30–60% AMI)

6 Apartments
(Below 30%)

Located in Edgartown, Massachusetts, in the heart of the New England summer resort Martha's Vineyard, Morgan Woods provides 60 affordable rental homes for year-round island residents who provide services essential to the success of the island. During the tourist season, these workers would typically have to live on the mainland and commute to work by ferry or rely on less-than-optimal housing strategies. Martha's Vineyard is similar to many resort communities with expensive housing, relatively low-paying jobs, and geographic development constraints. Morgan Woods represents a model for communities seeking to provide housing for resort workers. Through a 99-year land lease, innovative zoning, and an attractive design that disguises the density as a single-family home, the Community Builders (TCB), the developer of the project, was able to provide housing for people with a mix of incomes. Six units are reserved for households making less than 30 percent of the area median income (AMI), 30 units for households making between 30 and 60 percent of AMI, and 24 workforce units for households earning 60 to 140 percent of AMI.

MORGAN WOODS

Community Information

Historic Edgartown, once a center of the
Massachusetts whaling industry and now a
summer resort, lies at the heart of the thriving
Martha's Vineyard tourist trade. As the largest
town on the island, with well over 3,000
residents, it functions as a commercial and
residential hub. It has a historic town center
with restored homes adjacent to beautiful
beaches. Like most summer tourist destinations, Martha's Vineyard experiences massive
population fluctuations; the *Martha's Vineyard
Gazette* estimates a sevenfold surge in population during peak season from about 15,000
to more than 100,000. The trend of dramatic
population surges most likely will continue
as more and more people discover Martha's
Vineyard and Edgartown.

Workforce Housing Problem

Increased demand for lodging from seasonal visitors has placed a severe strain on the housing
supply. In recent years, year-round island residents—the teachers, nurses, municipal employees,
and shopkeepers who fuel the local economy—have found it increasingly difficult to find year-
round affordable housing on the island. A 2005 study by the Martha's Vineyard Commission
found that local residents earn 30 percent less than residents on the Massachusetts mainland and
that the cost of living and housing are 60 and 96 percent higher, respectively, than the national
average. Modest two- to three-bedroom ranch houses sell for well in excess of $500,000. Residents
who rent often must leave the island during peak tourist season, live on the mainland, and take
the ferry to jobs on the island, only to move back to the island once the season wanes and more
affordable rental rates return. Even those fortunate enough to own their homes often rent them

out in the summer months in order to afford the high cost of living on the island. Morgan Woods, an innovative public/private partnership between Edgartown and TCB, doubled the town's supply of affordable housing for permanent residents. With 60 units, it is the largest affordable housing development in the history of Martha's Vineyard.

Community Response

In 1998, recognizing the growing housing challenge for full-time residents and compelled to curtail the transient lifestyle deleterious to the health of the community, local residents rallied to the cause. Edgartown's Board of Selectman dedicated a 12-acre parcel of town-owned land for new affordable housing. After an extensive and competitive request-for-proposals process, the

town, with considerable citizen input, in 2004 selected TCB to finance, develop, and manage the Morgan Woods project.

Project Specifics and Affordability

Morgan Woods opened in May 2007, composed of 60 residential units on 12 acres divided among 21 buildings in an architecturally attractive and unique cluster setting. All are rental units, ranging from one to three bedrooms, with 24 designated as workforce and 36 as low-income housing. The 36 low-income tax-credit units will remain affordable for at least 30 years; of these, six units are dedicated to those earning less than 30 percent of AMI and 30 to those earning between 30 and 60 percent of AMI. Low-income units—defined as those dedicated to people earning up to 60 percent of AMI—start at $639 monthly rent for a one-bedroom unit and reach $861 for a three-bedroom unit. The remaining 24 units are dedicated to those in the workforce earning 60 to 140 percent AMI. In determining workforce affordability rates, TCB and Edgartown decided to include families earning up to 140 percent of AMI because the highly volatile, seasonal rental market made it difficult to extrapolate a standard market rate. One-bedroom workforce unit rents start at $1,239, two bedrooms at $1,475, and three bedrooms at $1,695.

Land and Site Acquisition

Edgartown and TCB formed a public/private partnership. They credit their success to a significant level of town participation and support, a 99-year ground lease, innovative zoning and site design, and a modular construction effort aligned with the tourist season. The 99-year ground lease, at a nominal annual cost to TCB, proved critical to making the project financially feasible for the developer and equally crucial in demonstrating the town's commitment to affordable housing. Edgartown was able to proffer a prime land parcel at such a low rate because of a mix of resident support and foresight. The town purchased a 180-acre parcel zoned for half-acre lots, then sold 120 acres to a conservation agency for the same price, effectively gaining 60 acres for free and allowing it to lease the 12-acre Morgan Woods site for a minimal rate.

Planning Entitlements and Development

The town led an intensive visioning process with local residents, leading to the ultimate design of the community. The town was deeply involved in the selection process, which culminated in the partnership with TCB and produced crucial local support. In working with TCB, Edgartown committed more than $400,000 for infrastructure improvements. The town also paid for numerous elements needed for the project, such as a site and program feasibility study, the environmental notification form, and a transportation study required by the regional commission. Edgartown agreed to a pay-in-lieu-of-

The town purchased a 180-acre parcel zoned for half-acre lots, then sold 120 acres to a conservation agency for the same price, effectively gaining 60 acres for free and allowing it to lease the 12-acre Morgan Woods site for a minimal rate.

Chapter 40B: Massachusetts's Comprehensive Permit Law

Massachusetts has set a goal of having 10 percent of the housing stock in each of its towns affordable to households earning 80 percent or less of AMI. In towns, Chapter 40B, often referred to as the Anti-Snob Zoning Law, allows compliant proposals to bypass local zoning ordinances to accommodate affordable units. Quite often, use of 40B is the only way to create any affordable housing in Massachusetts.

Legislators in Massachusetts approved Chapter 40B in 1969 to address local regulatory barriers to the construction of low- and moderate-income housing, and little has changed over the past four decades. To qualify for approval under Chapter 40B, a development must be approved or funded by an affordable housing program administered by a state agency, federal agency, or private housing trust fund. The development must have long-term affordability controls—more than 15 years—on at least 25 percent of the units. These units must be priced for families earning 80 percent or less of AMI. Developers must be a nonprofit organization, a quasi-governmental agency, or a limited partnership that agrees to cap profit at 20 percent.

taxes deal capping annual real estate taxes for the first 15 years of operations. Because the project was initiated by and for local citizens and involved them throughout its duration, the permitting and approvals process garnered high levels of support through a virtually unanimous vote that drew no appeal.

Financing

TCB structured a sophisticated financing strategy composed of state low-income housing tax credits, and 4 percent federal low-income housing tax credits and associated tax-exempt bond

Developers who qualify and invoke Chapter 40B enjoy a streamlined, alternative approval process. Chapter 40B overrides local zoning ordinances. The local zoning board of appeal (ZBA) of any town not meeting the 10 percent affordability standard must approve any project meeting the developer requirements, but can impose conditions on the project, provided the conditions do not make it uneconomic. If a ZBA rejects an affordable housing proposal under Chapter 40B or imposes conditions that render the project uneconomic, the developer can appeal to the state's Housing Appeals Committee (HAC).

Since the inception of Chapter 40B, almost 30,000 housing units have been built in more than 200 jurisdictions. About 34 percent of all affordable units in Massachusetts were constructed under Chapter 40B regulations. Despite the program's success, the state remains below its goal of each community having 10 percent of its housing stock affordable. Unless a community monitors its affordable supply constantly, it can be hard for it to avoid having Chapter 40B invoked against it if an affordable housing developer so chooses.

financing. In addition, the $16 million total development cost included soft sources from the state: a $750,000 grant from the Housing Stabilization Fund, $1 million in Affordable Housing Trust Fund money through the Massachusetts Housing Finance Agency (MassHousing), and $1.8 million from MassHousing's new Priority Development Fund. MassHousing's tax-exempt bond financing supported $4.9 million in permanent debt and $3.3 million in bridge financing. Wainwright Bank provided a $10 million construction loan. Apollo Housing Capital proffered $6.7 million in tax-credit equity financing.

Critical to gaining the necessary state tax credits and financial assistance, TCB had to demonstrate the worth and value of Morgan Woods in view of Massachusetts's highly competitive environment for housing resources. Because of the shortage of labor on Martha's Vineyard and the fact that materials must be ferried to the island, housing often costs at least 25 percent more than it does on the mainland. Faced with competition from other housing projects for state funds and subsidies, TCB had to construct Morgan Woods at a cost comparable to that of other areas in Massachusetts. To counter the location and labor cost disadvantage, TCB used modular housing design, which enabled it to maintain a consistent and predictable production schedule and complete the project on time and on budget. TCB used barges and built the project during the off season so as not to compete for transport capacity and labor during the tourist season. The use of modular components and off-season freight helped TCB build the units for $166 per square foot and stay competitive with other projects on the mainland.

Design, Planning, and Sustainability

With the town's support and financing in place, the partnership had to address the site's zoning and design. The existing zoning allowed half-acre lots yielding 24 homes on the 12 acres—two dwelling units per acre, far fewer than needed. To address the problem, the town used Massachusetts's innovative statewide Chapter 40B zoning laws, which permit developers to exempt affordable housing projects from local zoning processes in certain situations. Local residents, businesses, the town's Board of Selectman, and TCB worked together to put in place the necessary zoning and secure entitlements allowing for a denser development.

The town and TCB implemented a unique cluster design that disguises density. Morgan Woods includes 21 buildings that resemble single-family homes. Their heights, building materials, and architectural styles mesh with historic Edgartown, yet they are not single-family homes. The 21 structures house 60 units ranging from one to three bedrooms, allowing the site to achieve a

Because of the shortage of labor on Martha's Vineyard and the fact that materials must be ferried to the island, housing often costs at least 25 percent more than it does on the mainland.

density of five dwelling units per acre while maintaining visual architectural compatibility with the broader community. The site layout clusters the units in three areas, each similar to a mini-neighborhood with its own landscaped common like a New England town center.

The design of Morgan Woods also aims to enhance the natural environment of Martha's Vineyard. All the units surpass Energy Star efficiency standards, thereby reducing energy consumption and expenditures. Sensitive siting aligned with the natural contours of the terrain maximizes open space and helps preserve the environment. A majority of the 180 acres the town purchased will be preserved as open space and conservation land, and the 12-acre Morgan Woods site incorporates setbacks and buffers. The site also lies near Edgartown's downtown, allowing residents to walk to jobs, businesses, shops, and the Vineyard Transit Authority bus line.

Management and Affordability Controls

The housing program includes a unit for a 24-hour on-site manager and maintenance superintendent. The low-income housing tax credits guarantee that the 36 low-income units will remain so for at least 30 years.

Replication

Many seasonal and resort communities worldwide grapple with the problem of a lack of affordable housing for their year-round residents and workforce. Edgartown's innovative approach to provide low-income and workforce housing for its permanent residents offers some lessons other tourist destinations can emulate. The use of modular housing materials and construction during the off season is applicable to locales that suffer from labor shortages and accessibility issues. The level of resident buy-in and ownership of this development also sets it apart. Building affordable housing is not easy, but having widespread local support can facilitate the process significantly. Arguably the most crucial element in Morgan Woods' success stems from the town owning the land and having the ability to convey site control at effectively no cost to the developer. While this element of Morgan Woods' development might seem to be the most difficult piece to replicate, many jurisdictions might have the opportunity to purchase land and sell off key parcels. More likely than not, local governments own surplus, underused property that could be creatively used to provide housing to the workforce that is needed to make the community function.

FINALISTS

THE 2008 J. RONALD TERWILLIGER WORKFORCE HOUSING MODELS OF EXCELLENCE AWARDS

2008

EDUCATION HOUSING PARTNERS LLC • SAN MATEO COMMUNITY COLLEGE DISTRICT

COLLEGE VISTA

SAN MATEO, CALIFORNIA

DEVELOPERS

Education Housing
Partners LLC,
Mill Valley, California

San Mateo Community
College District,
San Mateo, California

**HOUSING
INFORMATION**

44 Rental Apartments

AFFORDABILITY

44 Apartments
Available to College
District Employees
(Rents Set at Level
of Affordability for
50% of AMI)

College Vista, a 44-unit rental housing project in San Mateo, California, is the product of a collaboration between a luxury apartment developer and a public community college district. Looking for a way to combat high employee turnover in one of the least affordable communities in the United States, the San Mateo County Community College District partnered with Education Housing Partners LLC (EHP)—an affiliate of Thompson|Dorfman Partners LLC—to develop workforce units available to college district employees at half the area median rental prices. Completed in December 2005, the financially self-sustaining development—rents at College Vista cover its operating expenses, finance costs, and a capital reserve—was achieved by developing the apartments on a surplus parking lot on the college campus, using tax-exempt debt financing through the issuance of certificates of participation (COPs) (see page 49), using a streamlined development process, and actively pursuing a community outreach program to overcome neighborhood opposition.

Community Information

San Mateo, a city of 93,000 residents, is about 30 minutes south of San Francisco and roughly the same distance north of San Jose. Located in San Mateo County, it is one of the larger suburbs in the Bay Area. An affluent community, the 2008 estimated median income for a household in San Mateo County was $95,000.

Workforce Housing Problem

Housing costs in San Mateo County are among the highest in the nation; four cities in the county rank among the ten costliest places in the United States to live. In 2003, the income required to purchase a median-priced home in the county was $173,000; today, that income requirement is more than $200,000.

Consequently, a lack of affordable housing has contributed to high employee turnover in the San Mateo County Community College District. In 2003, a survey conducted by the college district revealed that 18 percent of employees planned to leave the district within three years, and of those planning to leave, 57 percent cited unaffordable housing as the primary reason. Recognizing that the inability to recruit and retain staff harms the quality of education provided at San Mateo County Community College, the district began to examine potential solutions to its workforce housing problem.

Community Response

Because employee salaries—for both teachers and staff—are significantly below the median income of the county, the community college district decided to help close the affordability gap in homeownership for its workers. However, the district did not want to rely on public tax dollars or encumber its capital or operating budgets to do so. To solve this problem, the district used its

A survey revealed that 18 percent of employees planned to leave the district within three years, and of those planning to leave, 57 percent cited unaffordable housing as the primary reason.

municipal financing power to issue certificates of participation. Similar to state revenue bonds, COPs traditionally are used to fund capital improvement projects—gymnasiums or building expansions, for example—but at College Vista the purpose was expanded to include workforce housing.

The self-sustaining financial model, coupled with the use of surplus land owned by the college district, drove the development costs of the project well below those associated with traditional development in the area. At a development cost of $213,636 per unit, the district was able to provide below-market rents to its employees, allowing workers the time and opportunity to save for a downpayment on a home. When they are ready to purchase a home, the district offers employees an interest- and payment-free $75,000 second loan to assist with the purchase, further narrowing the affordability gap.

Project Specifics and Affordability

College Vista, situated on a hilltop on the grounds of the College of San Mateo, has 44 apartments configured in units of one bedroom, renting for $800 to 900; two bedrooms, at $1,100 to $1,250; and three bedrooms, at $1,350 to $1,450. The units range in size from 735 to 1,218 square feet,

depending on the number of bedrooms. All of the 44 units are rented, and there is a long waiting list for interested college district employees.

The district is statutorily required to lease four units at below-market rental rates; however, all the units are leased at levels that are affordable to very-low-income households earning less than 50 percent of the area median income.

The residential community is a ten-minute walk from a neighborhood shopping center with restaurants, services, and a grocery store. The college campus itself offers a wide variety of recreational, artistic, and social events ranging from a large fitness center to a farmers' market. The site is served by three major highways—State Route 101 to the east, Highway 92 to the south, and Interstate 280 to the west—and San Mateo County Transit District (SamTrans) buses and the Caltrain commuter rail system offer nearby public transportation options.

At College Vista, all 44 residential units are available to employees who do not own their own homes. Reduction of the amount of income spent on housing—College Vista rents are less than half market-rate levels—allows college district employees to save money for a downpayment on a home. By living on campus, they are able to save on commuting expenses as well.

When employees are ready to purchase a home, the college district offers a mortgage assistance program in the form of an interest- and payment-free $75,000 soft second loan. No payments—interest or principal—are required on the soft second mortgage for the first five years; 4 percent interest is charged from years five to ten; and at year ten, the loan is due and the district takes a proportional share of the appreciation of the home over the ten years. The district also offers $2,000 in downpayment assistance with no repayment required.

By providing an incentive for employees to purchase homes and offering temporary housing at half the market rate, the college district achieves two important goals: providing workforce housing in an expensive market and improving staff recruitment and retention.

Land and Site Acquisition

The 2.3-acre site is situated on part of a former overflow parking lot at the College of San Mateo campus. The project area was owned by the college district, eliminating the cost of land from the development's costs, which contributed to the project's affordability.

The project abuts a church property to the southeast and a luxury single-family neighborhood, separated by hard and soft landscaping, to the south. To the northwest, an administrative building adjoins the property, and a large open space is adjacent to the east.

Planning Entitlements and Development

College Vista was the result of an extensive outreach campaign, particularly with the residents of the adjacent single-family neighborhood who were concerned about affordable housing being built nearby. After identifying the potential issues, EHP partners and college district staff conducted a series of meetings with community members to address concerns, which focused on design

Part of a former overflow parking lot at the College of San Mateo, the project area was owned by the college district, which contributed to the project's affordability.

modifications and operating guidelines that would ensure the long-term quality of the project. In the end—and largely due to the strong community support—College Vista was quickly approved by the city of San Mateo.

Financing

Development of College Vista required an innovative collaboration among a public community college district, a luxury apartment developer, a planning and architecture firm specializing in multifamily housing, and a financial consultant to facilitate an imaginative method to finance and develop the workforce housing project. A turnkey development, College Vista was developed by EHP for the district and handed over to a nonprofit organization for property management.

The college district, as a public entity, exercised its municipal power to use certificates of participation to finance College Vista. Using COP financing—essentially tax-exempt bonds that offer favorable interest rates—allows a school district to finance capital improvement projects with little or no impact on its budget. The repayment and financing terms are structured, and COP financing has the added benefit of not requiring a public referendum, because technically the college district is not taking on debt. At College Vista, the rents cover the project's operational costs and principal and interest on the tax-exempt bonds, and fund a capital reserve.

Due to the financing structure and the use of surplus land, the project cost much less to develop than a conventional apartment project: all hard and soft costs were 100 percent capitalized through tax-exempt financing; municipal fees were reduced and school fees and property taxes were eliminated due to ownership by the college district; and the developer, project consultants, school district, and municipality worked together for cost-effective implementation. Also, the developer's fees were about 3 percent, as opposed to a more typical 6 percent, and the overall soft costs were about 50 percent less than for traditional development.

Certificates of Participation

In June 1978, California voters amended the state constitution through Proposition 13, the famous ballot initiative that began a nationwide discussion and has had a profound effect on the state. Although the centerpiece of the proposition was its cap on property taxes at 1 percent of the cash value of the property, it had other provisions as well. It required that issuance of a general obligation bonds requires a two-thirds majority vote of those living within the affected area. One implication of this provision is the emergence of what are known as certificates of participation (COPs). COPs are a method of funding used by governing agencies for the construction or improvement of public facilities. Because this type of funding uses a lease-type repayment structure, California law does not recognize the monies distributed as public debt. Federal tax law, however, views these types of obligations as debt, allowing for tax-exempt interest to the underwriter.

Through a COP, a public agency enters into a tax-exempt lease with a lessor that can be as long as 30 years. A COP obligates the general fund. COPs are used in California by school districts for construction or improvement of public facilities; the purchase of equipment such as buses, computers, etc.; and for refinancing existing leases. Because no voter approval is needed, COPs represent a quicker form of funding than general obligation bonds. This innovative use of financing not only provides much-needed funds to provide teacher housing, but also plays an important role in the public education system.

EHP's experience and comprehensive project management streamlined the project, building in more affordability by reducing development time frames and carrying costs. Additional funds were provided by a local utility company for mechanical upgrades that enhanced energy efficiency, and the redevelopment authority contributed funds that abated certain municipal fees.

Design, Construction, and Sustainability

The design team strived to create an attractive, high-quality building type and a site design that would foster social interaction among residents—all while respecting the sensitive coastal environment. The buildings feature craftsman-style architecture—tapered columns, articulated gable and shed forms, exposed beams, and vertical battens. Individual unit amenities include large floor plans, decks and patios, washer/dryers, private garages, and views of the mountains and bay.

At the center of the apartment complex is the community building, where residents can convene. The college district also uses the community room for retreats, meetings, and social events. In addition, the neighboring church and condominium homeowners association hold regular meetings at the facility, fostering a sense of community beyond the college campus.

The development, which transformed an impervious parking lot into a landscaped, attractive community, uses a number of sustainable practices: drought-tolerant plants reduce the need for irrigation; low-impact site design ensures that all stormwater is drained, collected, and treated on site; and increased insulation and energy-efficient heating, venting, and air-conditioning systems reduce energy use. Also, the on-campus location of the housing reduces overall greenhouse gas emissions: the college district estimates that about 150,000 commuter miles are saved each year because most staff and faculty would otherwise be forced to live well outside San Mateo and endure long commutes to work.

Management and Affordability Controls

A nonprofit foundation administers and manages College Vista to ensure that no conflict of interest arises from the college district being both the employer and landlord to its workers, while still allowing the public education district to control the future of the property.

Staff and faculty of the community college can rent units at College Vista for half the area median rent for five years. At that point, they must allow another eligible household on the

waiting list to move in. Because the rental housing is controlled by the college district, there are no problems with retaining affordability.

The district has also been able to use College Vista for recruitment purposes. For instance, a prominent science professor was recruited from Los Angeles with an offer that included a rental unit at the housing community.

Replication

As the second successful example of EHP's workforce housing template—Casa del Maestro in Santa Clara being the first—College Vista further validates this model, which could be used across the country to provide affordable rental housing for teachers, faculty, and staff members at schools and universities, with the added benefit of boosting employee retention rates. In addition, College Vista shows how surplus land and COP funding can be used to create workforce housing for moderate-income workers in a high-cost housing market.

CATELLUS DEVELOPMENT GROUP

MUELLER

AUSTIN, TEXAS

DEVELOPER

Catellus Development
Group,
Denver, Colorado

**HOUSING
INFORMATION**

2,200 Single-Family
Detached Houses
and Townhouses
(at Buildout)

2,400 Multifamily
Homes (at Buildout)

AFFORDABILITY

1,150 of the Homes Will
Be Income Restricted

For-Sale Homes
(up to 80% of AMI)

Rental Homes
(up to 60% of AMI)

Located in east Austin, Texas, a historically disadvantaged area of the city, Mueller is a large planned unit development on the site of the former municipal airport. The city partnered with ROMA Design Group and the Catellus Development Group to produce an innovative plan that is transforming the brownfield into a sustainable new urbanist community. With 20 percent green space, significant amounts of retail, office, and civic space, and plans to accommodate 10,000 workers and 10,000 residents, Mueller is a catalyst for the renewal of east Austin.

Community Information

Austin, with almost 750,000 residents, is the heart of a booming metropolitan region of more than 1.6 million people. As the state capital, Austin houses politicians, lobbyists, lawyers, and many other people with government-related jobs. It has also evolved into a sizable technology center, earning it the nickname "Silicon Hills." With the flagship campus of the University of Texas, Austin includes a bustling academic community of professors and students. Austin is also world renowned for its dynamic local music scene. Austin offers a very high quality of life and a diverse economy for its residents.

Workforce Housing Problem

The buzz around Austin is supported by its burgeoning growth. People want to live there and have migrated to the city in droves, making it the third-fastest-growing large city in the nation from 2000 to 2006. Rapid economic growth is often accompanied by a host of other issues, including traffic congestion, school crowding, and rising home prices. While Austin's developers and planners have tried to meet increased demand for housing through new supply, they have been unable to keep up with the growing need for homes. Housing prices increased 34 percent from 2000 to 2005. About 14 percent of Austinites live in poverty.

Community Response

Austin has made a concerted effort to address the issue of housing affordability. While the city has its share of public housing, it sought a better model for providing housing to families across all income groups. It created a unique housing policy initiative known as SMART—Safe, Mixed-income, Accessible, Reasonably priced, Transit-oriented housing—that aims to stimulate the production of new affordable housing for low- and moderate-income residents (see page 58). Developers who choose to work within the SMART guidelines receive expedited permit processing and fee waivers.

Project Specifics and Affordability

Located just three miles east of downtown Austin on the 711-acre site of the former Robert Mueller Municipal Airport, Mueller is a massive, mixed-income, mixed-use master-planned development. Currently, the master plan allows 4,600 new housing units for about 10,000 residents, 3.8 million square feet of commercial space, 650,000 square feet of retail space, a town center, a transit center, and 140 acres of open space. The housing ultimately will include 2,200 single-family

Located just three miles east of downtown Austin on the 711-acre site of the former Robert Mueller Municipal Airport, Mueller is a massive, mixed-income, mixed-use master-planned development.

"We are excited about the quality of these workforce housing projects. All the winning developments included a public/private partnership that is crucial in providing housing for the workforce. Through the awards program we hope to raise awareness of the possibilities for building workforce housing by showcasing exemplary developments, like Mueller." Bob Larson

detached homes and townhouses, as well as 2,400 multifamily units. Currently 200 single-family homes are occupied, and an additional 150 single-family units are under construction. A first phase of about 440 multifamily units is also under construction.

Mueller's master developer, Catellus Development Group, has committed to making 25 percent of all planned units, both rental and for sale, affordable. For-sale homes will be priced to be affordable for households earning up to 80 percent of the median family income (MFI). Affordable rental units will be reserved for those earning up to 60 percent of MFI. For-sale home prices will range in price from $120,000 to the $160,000s for affordable homes and from the $160,000s to over $1 million for market-rate homes.

Land and Site Acquisition

Opened in 1936, Robert Mueller Municipal Airport served Austin for many decades. However, as Mueller became increasingly hemmed in by development in the 1970s, Austin officials and residents began discussing the possibility of building a new airport to better serve the growing region. In 1991, voters approved a measure authorizing construction of a new airport. With a new airport in the planning stages, the city had to determine what to do with its valuable and soon-to-be-vacant 711-acre asset. Austin owned the entire Mueller site and had complete control over its disposition.

Planning Entitlements and Development

Austin formed a citizens' task force and hired ROMA Design Group in 1997 to develop a master plan for the site. Mueller Airport closed in 1999, and the city approved the ROMA master plan in 2000. After conducting an extensive nationwide search, Austin selected Catellus Development Group as the master developer, then began negotiations regarding the Mueller master development agreement.

In 2002, after much resident involvement, Austin adopted the master development agreement and applied appropriate zoning changes to the site in accordance with the site master plan. As a large, planned unit development converted from an airport, Mueller required more than 100 variations from the standard city code in order to become a high-quality, dense, mixed-use community at a reasonable cost. The city also built in evolutionary zoning provisions to accommodate the master plan and enable the density to increase in response to future market demand. Under Austin's SMART Housing program, Mueller homes also qualified for reduced permit fees and expedited reviews.

Mueller required more than 100 variations from the standard city code in order to become a high-quality, dense, mixed-use community at a reasonable cost.

Financing

In order to make the project financially feasible, both the city and Catellus contribute financially toward carrying out the master plan.

As master developer, Catellus relies on private financing to fund infrastructure construction. Catellus is reimbursed for these improvements by the city, which defers its proceeds from land sales and issues debt supported by project-generated property and sales tax revenues. Land sales to third parties also contribute to the funding of costs.

At the end of the redevelopment, there will be a final accounting, and Catellus will realize its investment returns through the money generated by land sales. The city also has the opportunity to share in land-sale proceeds.

Design, Planning, and Sustainability

It took the city and ROMA Design three years to develop a master plan and an additional two years for the city and Catellus to sign off on a master development agreement. As the largest redevelopment project in Austin's history, Mueller's sheer scale and scope necessitated tremendous long-range visioning and planning. Mueller's master plan aspires to achievement of several goals: fiscal responsibility; economic development; revitalization of the broader east Austin area; sustainability; diversity and affordability; and compatibility with the surrounding area.

The master plan incorporates a diverse mix of uses and a variety of building types and sizes.

Austin's SMART Program

Austin's SMART Housing Initiative is an innovative, self-funding program designed to increase the supply of affordable housing in Austin. The city uses an expedited review process and a sliding scale of fee waivers to encourage development that achieves SMART's goals of providing those elements that make up its acronym—Safe, Mixed-income, Accessible, Reasonably priced, and Transit-oriented housing. Austin created SMART in 2000 after an extensive planning and public review process designed to address the pattern of sprawl in the broader region by making housing development within the city competitive with the suburbs. SMART Housing incorporates three incentives to facilitate urban development: development fee waivers, expedited review by a designated team of SMART Housing staff, and assistance from that staff to resolve any development-related issues with other city departments.

In order for a project to receive SMART Housing designation and the incumbent incentives, a project must meet the following criteria:

■ Mixed-income/reasonably priced—a portion must be affordable for households earning up to 80 percent of AMI and spending no more than 30 percent of their family income on housing.

A central transit boulevard offering access to bus, rapid bus, and possibly light-rail transit will traverse the community; the vast majority of residents, employees, and shoppers will be no more than a ten-minute walk from mass transit. The residential units will rely on new urbanist principles and include elements such as porches, alley-loaded garages, apartments over retail, and an average density of 12 units per acre, with other uses reaching even higher densities. Every residence will be within 600 feet of a park or open space, which comprises 20 percent of the total site. Street trees along every street will

- Safe—compliance with the city's land development and building codes.
- Accessible—compliance with federal, state, and local accessibility standards.
- Transit—a location near a major or proposed bus route or light-rail line.
- Green—conformance to a minimum level of Austin's green building standards.

Developers who meet Austin's SMART standards receive a percentage fee waiver proportional to the total number of reasonably priced units. If 10 percent of the units qualify as SMART reasonably priced, the developer receives 25 percent fee waivers and fast-track review. If 20 percent qualify, the waiver is 50 percent; if 30 percent qualify, the waiver is 75 percent; and if 40 percent qualify, then all the fees are waived. Fee waivers are currently limited to 1,000 housing units and are allocated on a first-come, first-served basis. Developments of four or fewer housing units are required to be 100 percent reasonably priced and SMART aligned to qualify for waivers.

The Austin Housing Finance Corporation (AHFC) and Neighborhood Housing and Community Development (NHCD) are responsible for coordinating and administrating the SMART Housing program. In just three years, more than 4,000 new housing units have been completed through the SMART Housing program, significantly more than the 325 units produced before SMART's implementation.

provide shade and bring nature into the community. The town center will function as the heart of the development and will offer about 300,000 square feet of street-level retail and restaurants with offices and multifamily units on top.

The plan emphasizes walkability and incorporates a road network that integrates with adjacent parcels and diverts traffic away from the residential areas. Mueller will also feature civic institutions and public amenities such as schools, 13 miles of hiking and biking trails and lanes,

> *"Mueller is one of the largest redevelopment projects in the country. With a total buildout of 4,600 units and 25 percent committed to be affordable, this project will create over 1,000 units of affordable housing in Austin—quite an impressive feat. The fact that the community is being built for sustainability makes it all the more worthy of recognition."* Bart Harvey

outdoor art, and a regional children's hospital. A total of 3.8 million square feet of commercial space will provide 10,000 permanent jobs. Mueller's master plan won the Charter Award from the Congress for the New Urbanism in 2001.

From a sustainability perspective, Mueller will transform a brownfield into a model green development. In addition to the 20 percent of the site dedicated to green space, the buildings themselves will use minimal amounts of energy. Mueller is a pilot project in the Leadership in Energy and Environmental Design (LEED) for Neighborhood Development program. All residential units will achieve at least an Austin Energy three-star rating, which is comparable to a LEED Silver rating; all commercial buildings will achieve at least an Austin Energy two-star rating.

Management and Affordability Controls

Austin and Catellus have put considerable thought into the issue of affordability and how to preserve it for the long term. In compliance with the master plan, Catellus has committed to 25 percent affordability for all rental and for-sale units. On the rental side, affordability will be preserved for 50 years after first occupancy, and at least 10 percent of each multifamily complex—25 percent total—will be reserved for households earning less than 60 percent of AMI. Owners/

managers of rental properties will have to conduct income certifications for new tenants, and residents will pay rents in line with Austin's SMART Housing program. Incomes will be recertified annually; should a tenant's income rise to 140 percent of AMI, the unit will no longer be considered affordable and a replacement unit must be leased.

On the for-sale side, buyers who make 80 percent or less of AMI must be income certified at purchase. The affordable homes will be architecturally indistinguishable from market-rate homes from the exterior. The fact they are somewhat smaller, have a reduced land price, and offer fewer premium fixtures and finishes enables the lower price point. A shared value-appreciation program in the form of a second lien will allow the subsidy to be captured when a homeowner sells the unit at market rate. The subsidy, along with a pro-rata share of the net gain, is returned to the innovative nonprofit Mueller Foundation, which can deploy these dollars to ensure that affordable units come on line in subsequent phases of development.

Replication

Though the magnitude and complexity make this project unique, it is not the only airport redevelopment project in the country. Most major industrial cities have large parcels of vacant brownfield properties that could be put back to productive economic use, including as workforce housing. Communities contemplating a massive site redevelopment can use Mueller as an effective model of a project with sustainable master plan incorporating a mix of uses and housing for families with a mix of incomes.

AVENUE 26 CONDOMINIUMS LLC • PHOENIX REALTY GROUP

PUERTA DEL SOL

EAST LOS ANGELES, CALIFORNIA

DEVELOPERS

Avenue 26
Condominiums LLC,
Los Angeles, California

Phoenix Realty Group,
Los Angeles, California

**HOUSING
INFORMATION**

165 For-Sale
Condominiums

AFFORDABILITY

40 Condominiums
(80–150% of AMI)

15 Condominiums
(80–120% of AMI)

5 Condominiums
(Below 80% of AMI)

105 Condominiums
(Market Rate)

Puerta del Sol, completed in March 2007, is a 165-unit condominium building in the Lincoln Heights neighborhood of East Los Angeles. Served by the city's Gold Line light rail, the redevelopment project provides housing for lower- and middle-income households and improves the city's poor jobs/housing balance. Part of a larger, master-planned redevelopment of the area, Puerta del Sol reuses land that previously was a contaminated industrial site and provides housing opportunity for those earning 80 to 150 percent of the Los Angeles area median income (AMI). Mortgage assistance is provided by city and state programs, opening homeownership opportunities to working families who otherwise would not have qualified for conventional loans.

Community Information

Puerta del Sol is located in the Lincoln Heights neighborhood of East Los Angeles, two miles northeast of downtown. The first-ring suburb—one of the oldest neighborhoods in Los Angeles—was once home to the city's wealthiest residents but gradually fell into decay, particularly after the Golden State Freeway was constructed through the middle of the district in the 1950s. Over the past five years, the mixed residential and industrial neighborhood has begun a transformation, with introduction of a redeveloped shopping district and new residential projects served by the Metro Gold Line light-rail system.

Workforce Housing Problem

Southern California continues to suffer from an acute shortage of workforce housing. In Los Angeles, the fourth-least-affordable U.S. city, only 20 percent of homes sold were affordable for those earning the area median income in the third quarter of 2008, according to the National Association of Home Builders/Wells Fargo Housing Opportunity Index. The housing-to-jobs ratio is also imbalanced, with many workers forced to search far from major employment centers to find affordable housing, adding to the region's legendary traffic congestion.

Community Response

A number of programs exist at both the city and state level to promote development of workforce housing. The Los Angeles Housing Department (LAHD) provides mortgage assistance through its low- and moderate-income purchase assistance programs, which provide purchase assistance funds to first-time homebuyers. Puerta del Sol was awarded a forward commitment of $3.75 million in Moderate Income Purchase Assistance (MIPA) Program funds from LAHD.

In Los Angeles, the fourth-least-affordable U.S. city, only 20 percent of homes sold were affordable for those earning the area median income in the third quarter of 2008.

At the state level, mortgage and downpayment assistance is available for qualifying families through the California Homebuyer's Downpayment Assistance Program, the American Dream Downpayment Initiative (ADDI) funds, the Building Equity and Growth in Neighborhoods (BEGIN) Program, and California Housing Financing Agency (CalHFA) programs, all of which are designed to help working families bridge the affordability gap.

Project Specifics and Affordability

Puerta del Sol consists of 165 condominiums in studio and one-, two-, three-, and four-bedroom configurations. The $45 million mid-rise building features ground-floor retail and live/work units that enliven the pedestrian experience and provide a mix of uses. Situated on a former industrial site, the 199,000-square-foot project is part of a 12-acre master plan to redevelop the blighted and abandoned area of Lincoln Heights. Nearby amenities include schools, a pocket park, health clinics, and the Broadway retail area. Adjoining the site is the Lincoln Heights/Cypress Park light-rail station, only two station stops from Union Station, which connects riders to the regional rail system and to downtown Los Angeles. The Gold Line also connects riders to nearby Pasadena, another job and retail center.

At Puerta del Sol, buyers who earn 80 to 150 percent of AMI—$75,800 for a family of four—are eligible for mortgage assistance programs offered by California and Los Angeles. Of the 165 units, 55 were purchased by buyers who tapped into the $3.75 million in mortgage assistance from the LAHD's MIPA program: 15 units were made available to buyers earning 80 to 120 percent of AMI, fulfilling the program's requirement; another 40 units were made available for households earning from 80 to 150 percent of AMI. Another five buyers—earning less than 80 percent of AMI—used the LAHD's Low Income Purchase Assistance Program. Eighty percent of the buyers—whose numbers include social workers, nurses, teachers, policemen, and small-business owners—are first-time homeowners.

Land and Site Acquisition

Acquired for $2.9 million, the 2.9-acre site formerly housed an abandoned warehouse/manufacturing facility. The project area was contaminated from its previous industrial use and required environmental remediation. The cleanup effort was more comprehensive than anticipated—for example, site work uncovered two-ton lead kilns buried on the site—and ultimately cost the developer $6.2 million.

In conjunction with the redevelopment, the city provided new public infrastructure in the area—light rail, new parks, improvements to the Los Angeles River, tree plantings, upgraded sewer systems, and new street lamps—that catalyzed redevelopment along nearby commercial corridors in Lincoln Heights, helping make the residential project more viable.

Planning Entitlements and Development

The condominium project is part of developer AMCAL Homes' master-planned redevelopment—known as the Avenue 26 master plan—of a 12-acre tract of abandoned industrial land in Lincoln

The cleanup effort was more comprehensive than anticipated—for example, site work uncovered two-ton lead kilns buried on the site—and ultimately cost the developer $6.2 million.

Heights. Comprising 534 units of seniors', workforce (including live/work lofts), and affordable housing; a child-care center; and 3,000 square feet of community-serving retail space, Avenue 26 helps transform a previously moribund site into a transit-oriented community serving moderate-income families.

To facilitate the larger redevelopment effort, the Los Angeles City Council initiated a rezoning of the site to encourage development adjacent to the light-rail station. The zoning change—the site originally was designated for industrial use—allowed residential development at a higher density, greatly enhancing the development potential. The city also granted the developer a conditional use permit to allow creation of a shared parking program for the retail, live/work, and residential

Genesis Workforce Housing Fund

The Genesis Workforce Housing Fund is the product of a unique partnership between Genesis LA Economic Growth Corporation and Phoenix Realty Group. Genesis LA Economic Growth Corporation is a not-for-profit organization established in 2000 with the mission of using innovative market-driven financing strategies to stimulate development projects in low-income communities. Phoenix Realty Group is a for-profit national real estate investment management and development firm specializing in urban and suburban infill real estate, including residential, mixed-use, and commercial real estate. Backed by institutional investors, including public pension funds, banks, and insurance companies, Phoenix Realty Group currently manages six private equity real estate funds representing $3 billion in real estate acquisition and development.

The Genesis Workforce Housing Fund is a $100 million private equity real estate fund that provides equity financing for the development of workforce housing and mixed-use and commercial properties in Greater Los Angeles. The fund invests in a wide spectrum of

guest parking. The reduced parking requirement lowered the construction costs of the underground parking garage. Because the surrounding area was mostly industrial, no adjacent residential properties were affected, which limited community opposition to the development.

Financing

Puerta del Sol was developed by Avenue 26 Condominiums LLC, a partnership between AMCAL Homes and Phoenix Realty Group. The $45 million condominium building was the first project in Los Angeles to receive investment from the Genesis Workforce Housing Fund, the nation's first institutional source of capital to focus exclusively on market-rate housing for middle-income households (see box, above). In practice, the private equity real estate fund, fully capitalized at projects: rental and for-sale housing, including condominiums, townhouses, lofts, single-family homes, and apartments. The fund received $57 million of initial investment money from institutional investors in April 2004 and was fully capitalized at $100 million one year later. The fund's equity will be leveraged to provide over $500 million worth of workforce housing, producing more than 2,100 new housing units throughout Los Angeles.

The fund was the first institutional source of funding for market-rate workforce housing. It focuses its resources on low- and moderate-income census tracts and rede-velopment areas located in the urban core that lack housing affordable to middle-income families looking for the convenience of urban living. The fund invests in all stages of devel-opment financing, from predevelopment to land acquisition and development financing with mezzanine and/or equity investments from $1 million to $20 million. Minimum project size is 30 units, with development costs anywhere from $3 million to $100 million. The fund has invested in the Pan American Lofts and Santee Village in downtown Los Angeles, and Puerta del Sol in the Lincoln Heights neighborhood of East Los Angeles, among others.

$100 million, provides financing to third-party developers for creation of workforce housing in Greater Los Angeles.

Design, Construction, and Sustainability

The art deco–inspired building has studio units (637 to 652 square feet), live/work units (1,264 square feet), and units of two bedrooms (1,000 to 1,277 square feet), three bedrooms (1,294 to 1,353 square feet), and four bedrooms (1,501 square feet), all arranged around a central courtyard. Developed at 57 dwelling units per acre, Puerta del Sol also has 3,000 square feet of ground-floor retail space and live/work units along the streetfront, creating a pedestrian environment. An under-ground garage provides 290 parking spaces—248 residential and 42 guest/retail shared.

The design team intended the interior and exterior features to rival luxury condominium projects elsewhere in the city: each unit has upgraded stainless-steel appliances, slab granite countertops in the kitchens and bathrooms, ceramic tile entries, and balconies. Community amenities are a professionally decorated clubhouse with a billiard room and kitchen, a fitness facility, and a landscaped courtyard with fountain. The complex is secure at all access points—the main entrance, courtyard entryways, the parking garage, and along Avenue 26.

Management and Affordability Controls

Puerta del Sol has been a financial success: it was the best-selling mid-rise in Los Angeles during summer and fall 2006, and averaged 4.2 sales per week and 17.5 per month over this time span. The original interested buyers list had 3,000 names.

Affordability of the workforce units is maintained through a variety of subsidized mortgage programs from both the city and the state. The loans—purchased by the 55 qualifying households—were acquired through the city's $3.75 million in mortgage assistance funds, and are repayable at the end of the term—30 years—or at the time of sale or transfer. The loans offered under the LAHD programs—ranging from $50,000 to $105,000—gave the buyers the purchasing power needed to become homeowners.

LAHD Purchase Assistance funds require equity sharing at resale, after a five-year owner-occupancy period. CalHFA can add an additional 3 percent of purchase price toward downpayment.

Replication

The use of demand-side subsidies—in the form of downpayment and mortgage assistance through various city and state programs—is a replicable model to bridge the financing gap many workforce households face. Also, the award of a forward commitment—essentially a contractual promise from the city to the homebuilder that mortgage assistance funds will be made available to potential homebuyers—is a replicable model for encouraging the development of workforce housing. This program allows the developer to market to an additional demographic of potential buyers who otherwise would be unable to afford a home. While the units were reserved as affordable, the entire project was considered market-rate housing because the forward commitment loans filled the gap between the market-rate sales price and the price affordable to the qualifying households.

TWELVE CENTENNIAL PARK

ATLANTA, GEORGIA

DEVELOPERS

Novare Group,
Atlanta, Georgia

Atlanta Development
Authority,
Atlanta, Georgia

**HOUSING
INFORMATION**

517 For-Sale
Condominiums

AFFORDABILITY

170 Condominiums
(80–120% of AMI)

104 Condominiums
(Below 80% of AMI)

240 Condominiums
(Market Rate)

Situated between Atlanta's bustling Midtown and downtown business districts, Twelve Centennial Park bridges the city's two largest employment centers while offering much-needed, affordable infill housing adjacent to mass transit. A partnership between the Novare Group and the Atlanta Development Authority (ADA), Twelve Centennial Park is a $134 million mixed-use, mixed-income development. Its hotel, street-level retail, office space, and 517 condominiums are expected to energize the area and help combat Atlanta's notoriety as a sprawling suburban mass. More important, it is offering 104 housing units for Atlantans earning 80 percent or less of the area median income (AMI) and 170 units for those earning between 80 and 120 percent of AMI. The Atlanta Neighborhood Development Partnership Inc. (ANDP) is managing the marketing, sales, and qualification of buyers for the affordable housing program.

Community Information

With more than 500,000 people in the core of a larger region of well over 5 million people, Atlanta has enjoyed a 38 percent population growth rate since 1970 and serves as the booming de facto capital of the New South. It has the busiest airport in the world and easy access to global markets. The site of the 1996 Summer Olympic Games and the headquarters of numerous corporations such as Delta and Coca-Cola, Atlanta possesses a strong, diverse economy.

Workforce Housing Problem

Part of Atlanta's image problem as a sprawling, land-devouring region stems from the fact that many of the families living in the growing exurbs cannot afford property closer to the core of the region. These "drive to qualify" buyers push metropolitan Atlanta's borders farther and farther out. According to ANDP, a local nonprofit housing organization, 63 percent of all jobs in the region pay less than $40,000 annually and one in three households earns less than $40,000 per year. ANDP reported that on average, 61 cents of every dollar Atlantans spend goes for housing and transportation expenses combined, second only to San Francisco.

Community Response

Atlanta has a variety of public agencies and nonprofit partners committed to affordable housing. The ADA serves as the official economic development entity for the city. It concentrates on residential, business, and investment growth and often partners with one or more of over 50 other economic development organizations. Among the ADA's focus areas, it offers several initiatives to make living in Atlanta affordable for various workers and families.

Project Specifics and Affordability

Twelve Centennial Park is part of a larger development known as Allen Plaza, a nine-block project on the northern edge of downtown. When built out, Allen Plaza will incorporate 2.5 million square feet of Class A office space, 250,000 square feet of retail space and restaurants, 2,500 residential units, and more than 1,000 hotel rooms, and will link to downtown assets such as Centennial Park and the Georgia Aquarium. Among the marquee tenants will be the W Hotel and Residences, Accenture, and the Southern Company. Twelve Centennial Park, a critical component of Allen Plaza, has 517 condominiums, a hotel, offices, and retail space sited on 3.75 acres. The high-rise structure achieves a density of 137 units per acre.

Of the residential units, 104 are affordable and 413 are market rate. The affordable units are priced for those earning up to 80 percent of AMI; one-bedroom units sell for $144,000 and

ANDP, a local nonprofit housing organization, reported that on average, 61 cents of every dollar Atlantans spend goes for housing and transportation expenses combined, second only to San Francisco.

two-bedroom units for $155,000. One hundred seventy of the 413 market-rate units are targeted at buyers earning 80 to 120 percent of AMI and have a price point approaching $242,000. The remaining market-rate units sell for $200,000 to $600,000.

Land and Site Acquisition
Twelve Centennial Park and the entire Allen Plaza property lie within one of Atlanta's tax allocated districts (TADs) (see page 78). A TAD functions similarly to a TIF district in that it can issue bonds to be repaid using tax revenues within the district and allocate funds raised by those bonds for improvements within the designated district. The ADA serves as the redevelopment agent for all Atlanta TADs. The Novare Group acquired the parcel for Twelve Centennial Park for $8.3 million in fall 2003, and residents began moving into new units in August 2007.

Planning Entitlements and Development
Located within Atlanta's Eastside TAD, Twelve Centennial Park came with an ADA mandate that in order to receive tax allocation funds, the project would have to include some affordable housing. Through the tax allocation, ADA was able to subsidize 20 percent of the units with "soft" second mortgages of about $100,000 per unit, enabling the Novare Group to incorporate the affordable units in a financially feasible way. The TAD provided for some infrastructure and site improvements as well, but the main benefit it offered was in the allocation of tax revenues in the soft second mortgage program to lower unit prices and guarantee that low- to moderate-income buyers could purchase 20 percent of the units.

Atlanta as a region has begun to embrace smart growth principles, specifically the idea of increased density and transit-oriented development. The Atlanta Regional Commission has implemented a development of regional impact (DRI) tool to measure the effects of large-scale development across the region rather than just within the development's jurisdiction. Novare

Atlanta Development Authority subsidized 20 percent of the units with "soft" second mortgages, enabling the Novare Group to incorporate the affordable units in a financially feasible way.

Tax Allocation Districts

Tax increment financing (TIF), which has existed since 1958, has helped spur redevelopment of blighted areas nationwide. Georgia employs a similar practice through its tax allocation districts (TADs). A TAD, similar to what many states refer to as a TIF district, is a geographic area in which TIF can be used as an economic redevelopment tool. Passed in 1985, the Georgia Redevelopment Powers Law granted local jurisdictions the power to redevelop economically depressed areas. One of the powers authorized is the use of tax allocation bonds to finance infrastructure improvements and redevelopment within a TAD.

Atlanta first approved establishment of TADs in 1986. In order to qualify as a TAD, an area must be assessed by the city and verified as needing redevelopment. In Georgia, unlike many states, approval of a TAD does not require a finding that an area is blighted. To be approved, a TAD must have a redevelopment plan that outlines why the area needs improvement and how the city plans to revitalize the district. The Atlanta Development

participated in the DRI intergovernmental review process and asked for five minor variances, but did not require any significant rezoning for this project.

Financing

In addition to receiving TAD funds in the form of infrastructure improvements and soft second mortgages, Novare used a first mortgage from GE Capital, as well as private equity from several sources.

Design, Planning, and Sustainability

Twelve Centennial Park has significantly enhanced Atlanta's urban core revitalization efforts. The high-quality design of the complex and its alignment with the larger Allen Plaza development

Authority (ADA) administers TADs within the city and issues TAD bonds for district improvements. TAD bond revenues must be used within the TAD's boundaries. A typical TAD lasts for 25 to 30 years, but can be cut short if the bond gets repaid earlier. Under the state's Redevelopment Powers Law, cities cannot create new TADs if the total value of extant and proposed TADs exceeds 10 percent of total taxable property value. Atlanta has reached this limit and cannot create any additional TADs.

TAD funds have wide applicability that can include construction of new buildings, demolition, and provision of infrastructure, among other uses. However, use of TAD funds must be consistent with the TAD's redevelopment plan and the bonds must be repaid with the tax increment over time. In Atlanta's Eastside TAD, site of Twelve Centennial Park, the ADA administered some of the funds in the form of a soft second mortgage. This use of TAD funds to allow some units to come to market at subsidized prices aligns with the redevelopment plan for the Eastside TAD.

add density and diversity to a key part of the city. With 517 residences, a 102-suite boutique hotel, 12,800 square feet of street-level retail space, 5,000 square feet of restaurant/bar space, and 12,500 square feet of office space, the project has catalyzed the area with a vibrant mixture of uses.

The planning of the site complements the existing and planned urban fabric of the area so that it integrates with its surroundings rather than being isolated. Residents can walk to numerous employers within the neighborhood and have direct access to the Metropolitan Atlanta Rapid Transit Authority (MARTA) light-rail line at the Civic Center station directly across from the project on West Peachtree Street. Such high density, combined with immediate access to jobs and transit, offers a major step forward in Atlanta's attempts to support transit-oriented development. Residents of Twelve Centennial Park have a greatly reduced need for an automobile. Not only does the development help lessen land consumption and commuter-generated greenhouse

gas emissions, but it also incorporates energy-efficient technology. All units and common areas use compact fluorescent lighting. Each unit also has its own submeter so residents can gauge their own utility use. All tenants will also participate in a development-wide recycling program.

Management and Affordability Controls

ADA partnered with ANDP to administer the TAD funds allocated for second mortgages. ANDP provides the soft second mortgage to buyers who meet the eligibility criteria. To qualify for soft-second-mortgage assistance, potential buyers must own no real estate, have a household income that does not exceed $56,950, and plan on making Twelve Centennial Park their primary residence.

"Twelve Centennial Park is a great demonstration of collaboration between public, private, and nonprofit organizations to address housing needs in downtown Atlanta. Offering 20 percent of Twelve Centennial Park's 517 units at affordable rates is a great commitment to mixed-income and workforce housing. The proximity of Twelve Centennial Park to our public transit rail system also adds tremendous value for residents who want to reduce their transportation expense and their carbon footprint. ANDP applauds Twelve developers Novare Group and the city of Atlanta Development Authority for their strong partnership."

John O'Callaghan, president and CEO, Atlanta Neighborhood Development Partnership

ANDP recovers its mortgage subsidy upon resale of the each subsidized unit. This repayment system creates a revolving stream of money ANDP can invest in other affordable units in the same TAD, but it does not ensure that the exact unit remains affordable.

Replication

Twelve Centennial Park offers an example of a high-quality, mixed-use development aligned with transit. Its density and mix of uses that complement the downtown and Midtown centers serve as a model for bridging two distinct nodes. The partnership with ADA and the use of soft second mortgages to accommodate affordable units is a practice that many developers and jurisdictions can emulate.